Oriental
Designs

SEARCH PRESS

First published in Great Britain 2009 by

Search Press Limited
Wellwood
North Farm Road
Tunbridge Wells
Kent TN2 3DR

Text copyright © Search Press 2009
Photographs by Debbie Patterson,
Search Press Studios
Photographs and design copyright ©
Search Press Ltd 2009

ISBN: 978-1-84448-441-6

The Complete Book of Oriental Designs is a
compendium volume of illustrations taken from the
Design Source Books: *Oriental Flower Designs*,
Chinese Designs, *Traditional Japanese Designs*,
Persian Designs

Printed in Malaysia

Page 1

Embroidered Iris: Kakitsubata

By Julia D Gray

Design, see page 60

Japan is known as the Land of Flowers. Gardens
are a place for viewing flowers and plants; they are
sometimes designed so that no foot should enter
there, especially in the moss gardens. Plants are
groomed and clipped, but it is the natural setting
which gives a chance for meditation, such as at the
O-Hana-mi Festival of 'viewing the flowers'. The most
perfect meditation is said to be on the opening of a
cherry blossom, from bud to full flower, which takes
one whole day. Flowers have great symbolism. Buds
and rolled-up leaves suggest the future, open flowers
symbolise the present and seed pods or drying leaves,
crinkled with time, represent the past.

The Iris is the symbol for Boys' Day Festival. The
blade-like leaf is thought to resemble the Samurai
sword and the flower is usually depicted in water to
show the strength of the plant against the flow of the
stream. A koi (carp) is often featured to also represent
strength and perseverance – a true warrior spirit.

For the flower, 2/1 flat silk is used – diagonally stitched
for the centre petals, and 4/1 twist is diagonally
stitched to the left and to the right, leaving one point
open space for the veins in the outer petals. For the
leaves, 2/1 flat diagonal stitching is used, starting at
the point and working down the leaves. It is important
for leaves to have nice points.

For the water, one pair of no 4 silver threads, couched
in white silk couching thread to give the feeling of
flowing water, which when it catches the sunlight
shines silver. This couching thread does not detract the
eye from that feeling.

Page 3

Glass Painted Geisha Girls

By Judy Balchin

Design, see page 51

Geisha girls are traditional Japanese entertainers
and the beautiful garments and accessories they wear
reflect their love of music and dance. Glass paints, with
their strong, vibrant colours, are ideal for this design
(see page 15).

Contents

Introduction 4

Project Ideas

Embroidered Iris
Kakitsubata   1

Parchment Craft Card   6

Vibrant Fan Cards   7

Dragon Plaque   8

Embossed Book Cover   9

Eastern Wall Plaques   10

Silk Painted Picture   11

Treasure Chest   12

Chinese Opera Mask   13

Fabric Painted Cushion   14

Glass Painted Geisha Girls   15

Glass Painted Vase   16

Designs 17

Introduction

The term Orient comes from the Latin word *oriens*, which means east. Initially, it referred to only Middle Eastern countries, but by the late nineteenth century, the Orient included Japan, China, Korea and surrounding nations. Today, it is a vast area and it includes a huge range of cultures. Because of this, design sources and styles are incredibly varied. There is no denying that Eastern artists created beautiful designs, whether depicted in decorative, realistic or stylised forms. Flowers, animals, birds and figures, with their distinctive styles are found in profusion in Eastern art, architecture, literature, textiles and ceramics.

Today, Oriental designs are as popular as ever. You only have to look in our high street stores to see how Eastern styles are used to sell jewellery, fashion fabrics, stationery, home furnishings and much more. Inspired by the rich source of material, this book offers patterns, motifs, borders and ideas for your own work. You do not need to be particularly artistic to use the designs. Just photocopy or trace the illustrations and transfer them on to your project pieces. You will soon discover the joy of making something beautiful for yourself or your friends and family.

To inspire you, the first section of the book offers an assortment of project ideas, including an embroidered iris by Julia D Gray plus a selection of craft projects designed by Judy Balchin. Images have been chosen from the design section of the book to illustrate how the motifs can be used to decorate different surfaces. Here you will find glass painting, silk painting, embossing, parchment craft, fabric painting and polymer clay work. Full instructions are not given for these items. However, if you feel tempted to create them or are inspired to learn one of the crafts shown in these pages, we offer a full range of technique books, with easy to follow step-by-step instructions, on our website: www.searchpress.com.

We wish you well. Have fun.

The Search Press Team

Opposite

For details of the three projects, turn to page 11 for the silk painted flower girl picture, page 10 for thc three Eastern wall plaques and page 12 for the treasure box.

Opposite

Parchment Craft Card

By Judy Balchin

Design, see page 17

Parchment paper is ideal for the delicate butterfly on this pretty card. The design is traced on to the surface of the parchment paper using pearlised ink, before being embossed with an embossing tool. Areas are then outlined and pricked with a pricking tool to add detail. The wings are bent upwards slightly. A thin strip of double sided tape is attached to the underside of the body, trapping a few strands of silver embroidery thread. The butterfly is finally pressed on to a base card layered with gold and patterned paper.

Vibrant Fan Cards

by Judy Balchin

Design, see page 31

Beautiful fan cards can be created with a few coloured pencils and some decorative background papers. The fans are photocopied, mounted on to thin card and coloured before being cut out and threaded with matching embroidery thread. The ready-made base card is layered with a square of floral paper. The circular hole is cut out and the fan is mounted across the hole using small sticky pads.

Oriental Dragon Plaque

By Judy Balchin

Design, see page 58

Historically, Eastern dragons are revered and loved, and they feature greatly in Eastern folklore. They symbolise power and heroism, and they are thought to bring good fortune. This dragon design is traced on to thin card and painted with orange, yellow and red gouache. The fiery colours give an impression of strength and the long plaque complements the graceful lines of the design. When the colours are dry, the design is outlined with a fine black felt-tipped pen. It is then backed with wood which has been decorated with hand-made papers and small painted wooden squares. Holes are drilled at each end of the plaque and threaded with leather thongs, and chains decorated with colourful pom pom and shell embellishments.

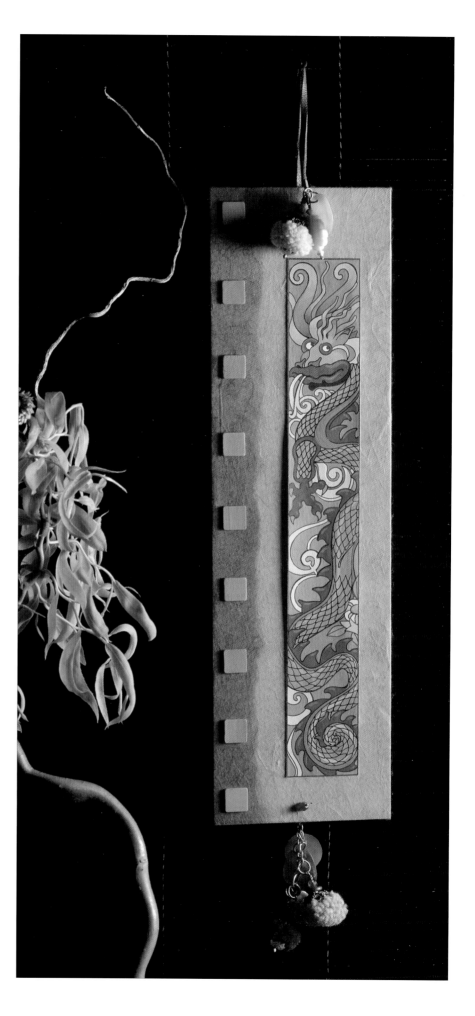

Embossed Book Cover

By Judy Balchin

Design, see page 76

Many of the designs in this book are ideal for metal embossed projects. This plain notebook is covered with floral paper. A strip of spotted paper is then wrapped around the spine and glued into place. The main floral design is embossed on to thin gold embossing foil, cut out and glued to the cover. The book is then wrapped with ribbons before being decorated with gold embellishments and gems.

Opposite

Eastern Wall Plaques

By Judy Balchin

Design, see page 57

There is a good selection of miniature designs on page 57 and they are ideal as decoration on small wall plaques. The images are outlined on circles of thick card using glass painting outliner to give raised lines. When the outlines are dry, the circles are pressed into polymer clay which has been rolled out flat. They are then cut out. A straw is used to remove small areas of clay at the top of each circle for the hanging holes. When baked, the circles are painted and rubbed over with gold or silver wax to give a metallic finish. Finally, they are threaded with leather thongs and beads.

Silk Painted Picture

By Judy Balchin

Design, page 53

Silk painting is closely associated with Oriental art. This flower girl is traced on to stretched silk before being outlined with gold outliner and painted with silk paints. To give the background an aged appearance, it is painted with pale yellow, and while still wet it is sprinkled with rock salt. As the colour dries it is pulled into the salt granules, creating a swirling, textured effect. The painted silk is stretched around a piece of thick card and taped securely on the back, before being mounted within the gold frame.

Oriental Treasure Chest

By Judy Balchin

Designs, pages 61 & 81

Beautiful flowers and bamboo leaves decorate this small treasure chest, which is painted initially with red acrylic paint. When dry, the bamboo foliage is added in black. The floral plaques are created with polymer clay. The designs are outlined on to card using glass painting outliner, to give raised lines. When dry, they are pressed into a sheet of rolled polymer clay and cut out. After baking, the plaques are painted with red acrylic paint, rubbed over with gold wax and glued to the box. Small dots of gold outliner are used to neaten the edge of the plaques and to add a little sparkle to the bamboo decoration.

Chinese Opera Mask

By Judy Balchin

Design, page 33

This painted mask was inspired by the designs on page 33. No particular design was actually copied. In Chinese opera, masks are used on stage to denote the different characters of the players. The colours of the masks also play a key role in portraying the differences. This ready-made mask is altered slightly by making the mouth and eye holes larger to give a fiercer appearance. Acrylic paints are then used to decorate the mask with swirls and waves of bright colour. When dry, dots of gold outliner add a dramatic touch

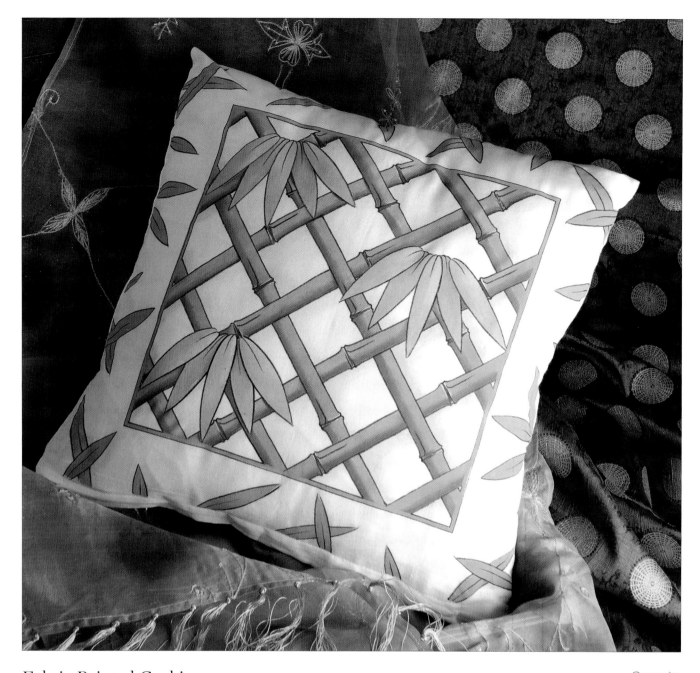

Fabric Painted Cushion

By Judy Balchin

Design, see page 25

This lattice-work bamboo design is used to transform a plain cotton cushion cover. The central design is lightly drawn on to the cover with a pencil, then painted with fabric paints. When dry, decorative bamboo leaves are added around the edge. Finally, the designs are outlined using a black fabric pen.

Page 16

Glass Painted Vase

By Judy Balchin

Design, see page 41

The floral design has been simplified slightly to fit on the glass vase. The design is taped to the inside of the vase, then the image is outlined on the outside surface using black outliner. When the design is dry, the vase is laid flat and painted with bakeable water-based glass paints. Once baked, the design is dishwasher safe and durable.

Opposite

Glass Painted Geisha Girls

By Judy Balchin

Design, see page 51

The Geisha girls, dressed in their elaborate kimonos, cry out for rich colour, so the strong outlines and vibrancy of glass paints are perfect for this design. The ready-made frame is disassembled and the design is taped to the underside of the glass, then the image is outlined on the top of the glass using black outliner. When the design is dry, glass paints are applied generously to each area, so that they settle flat to produce a smooth finish. The painted glass is backed with cream card before the frame is reassembled.

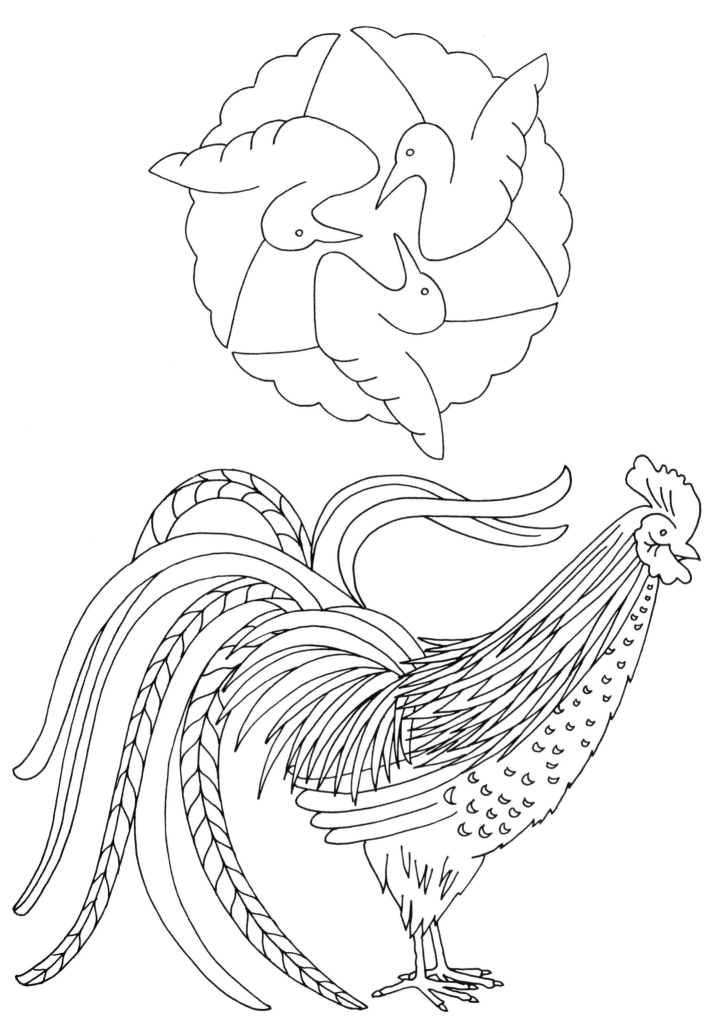

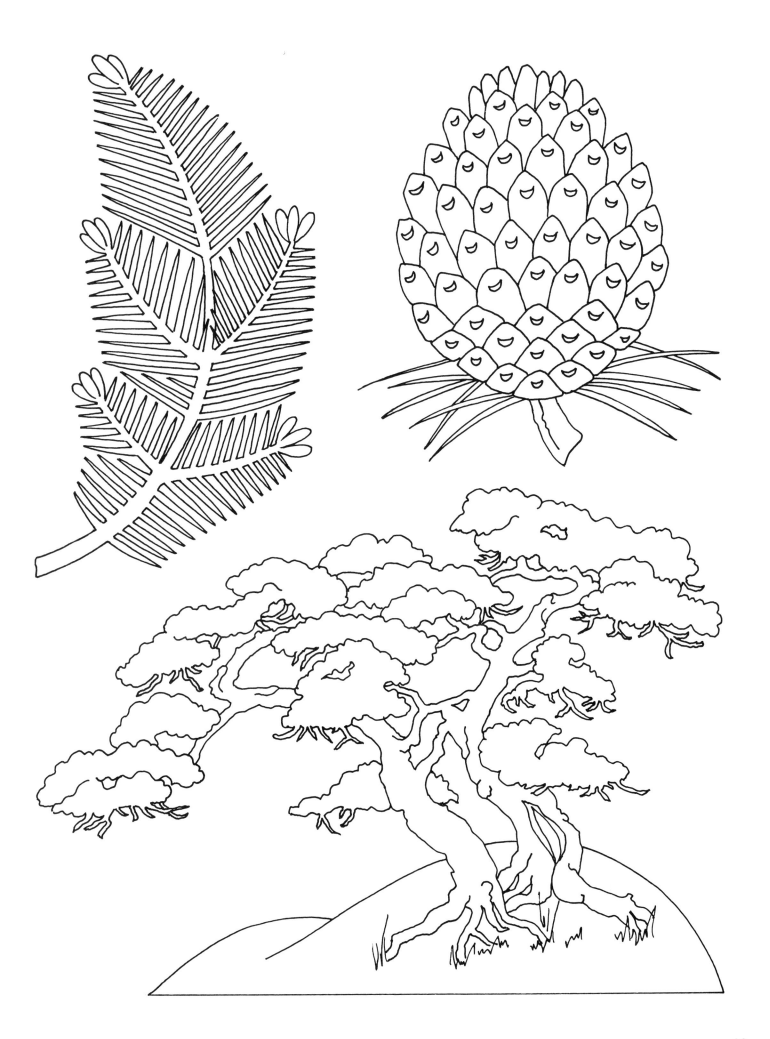

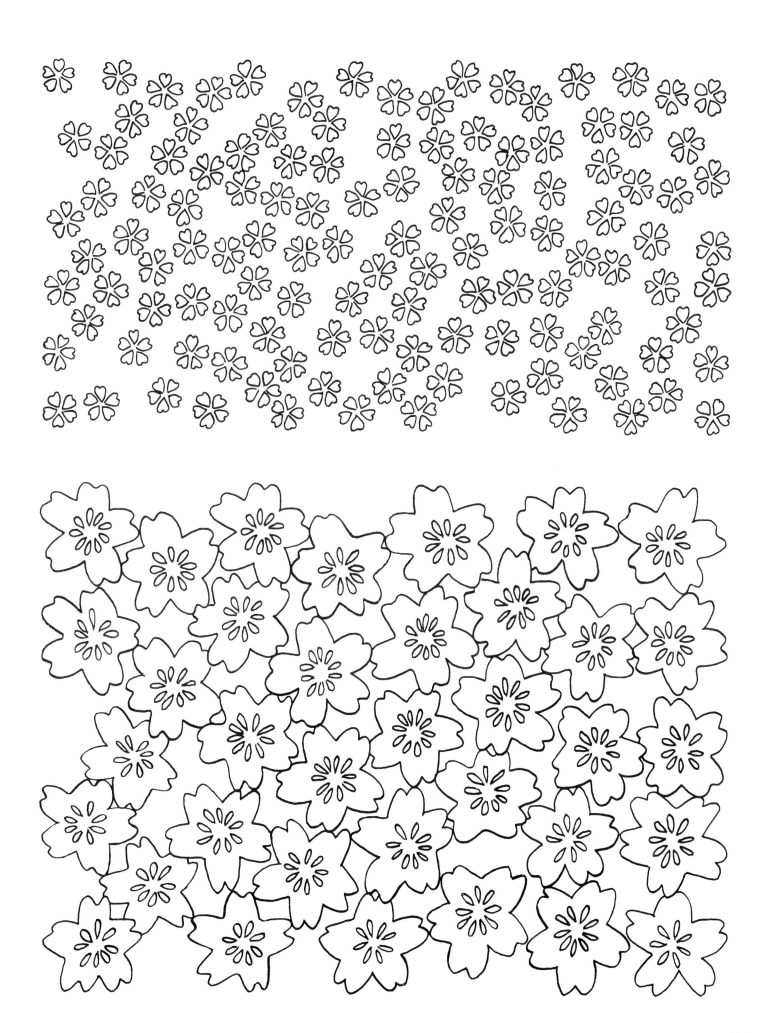

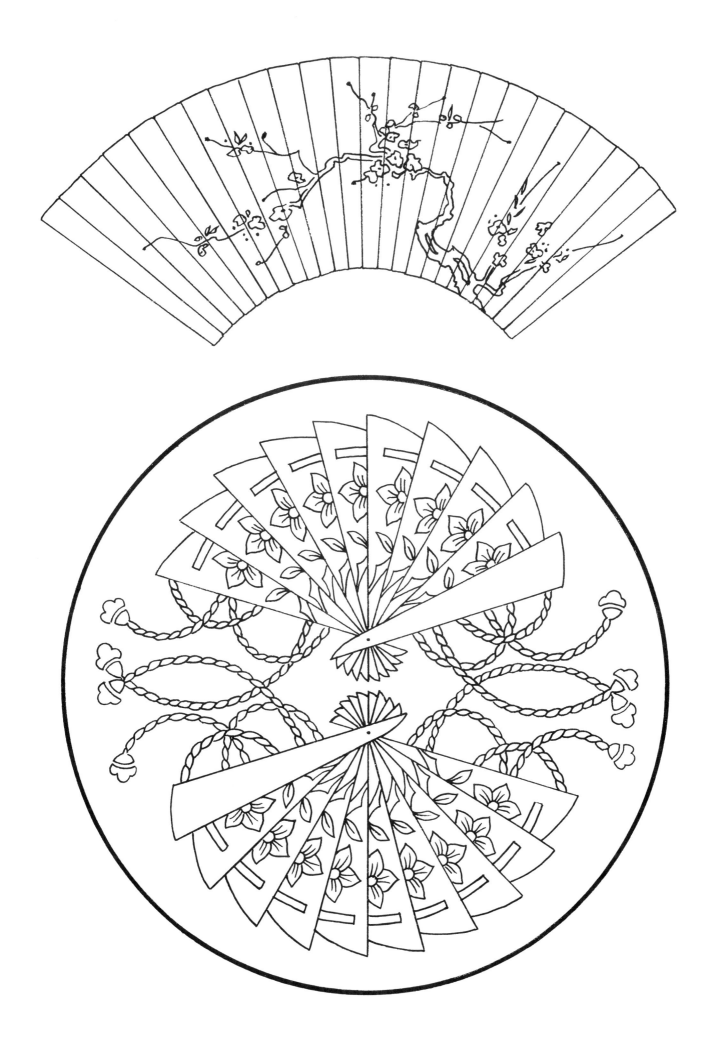

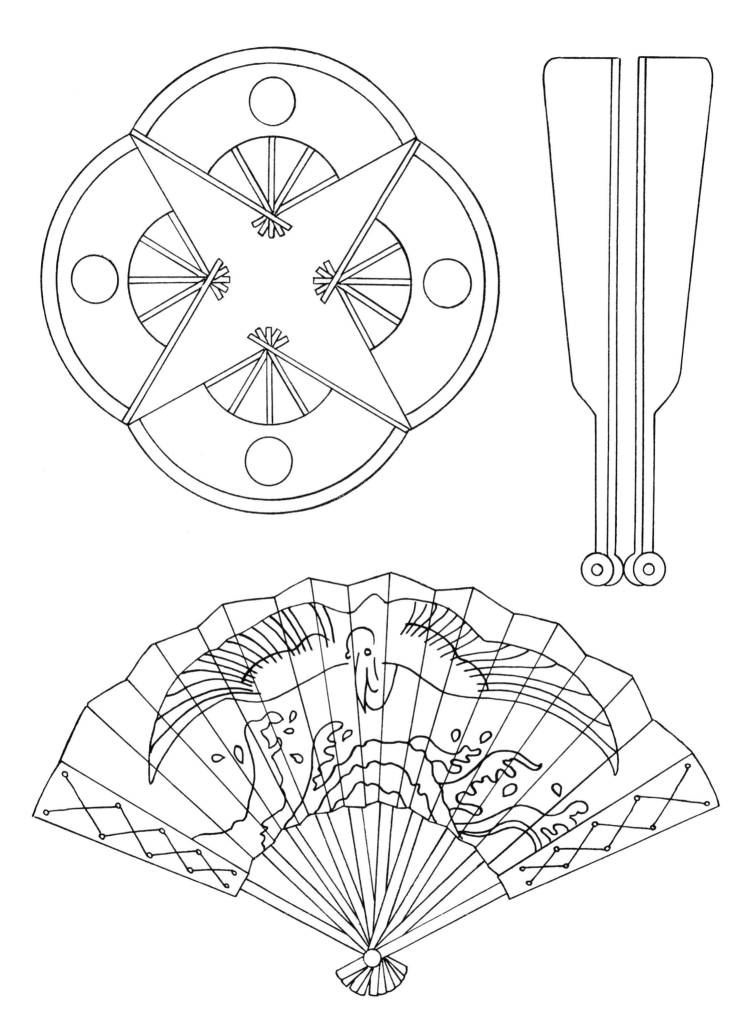

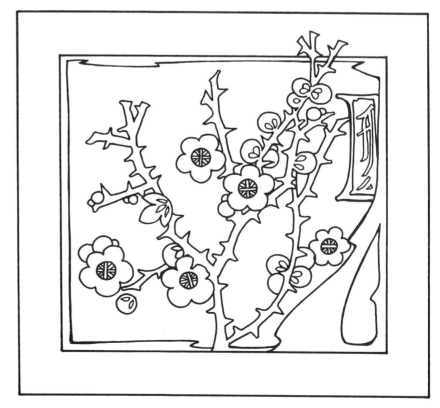

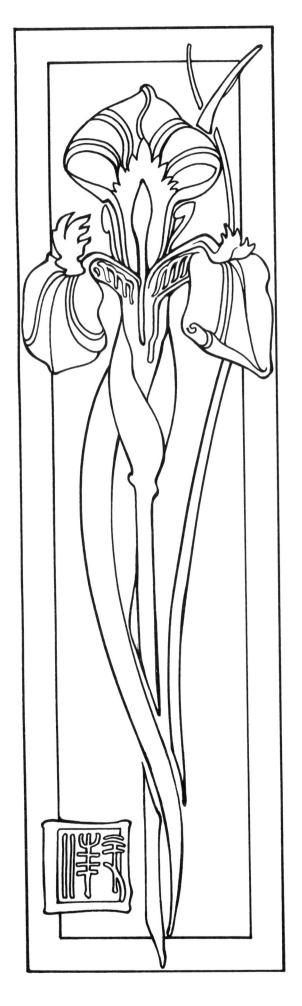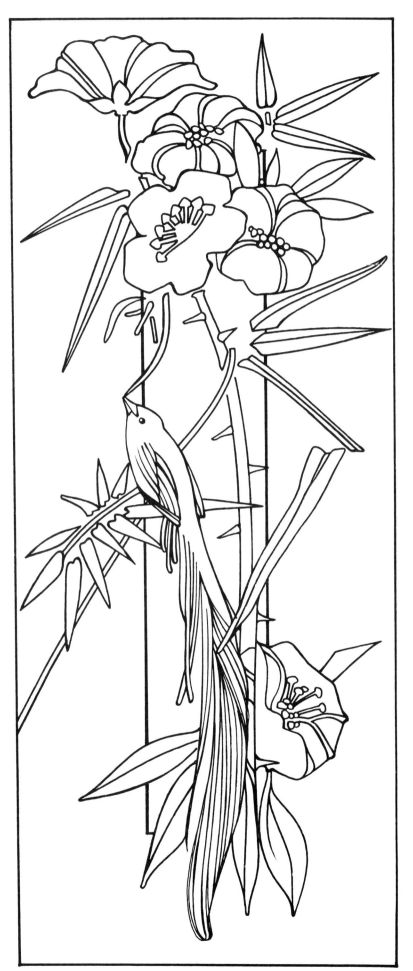

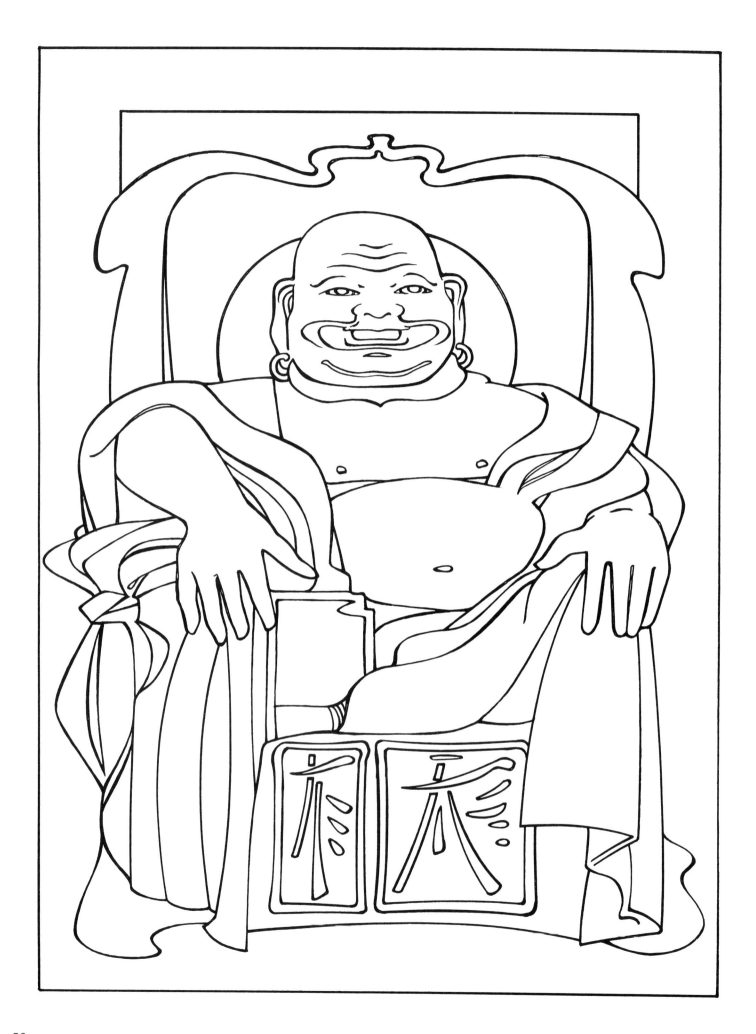

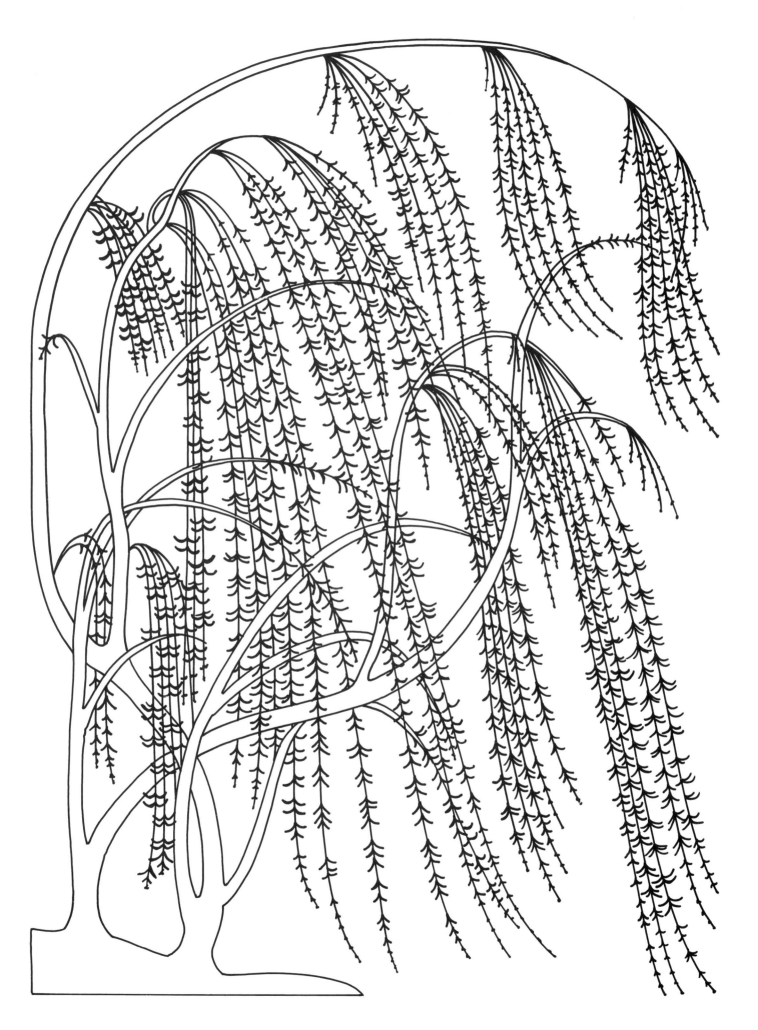

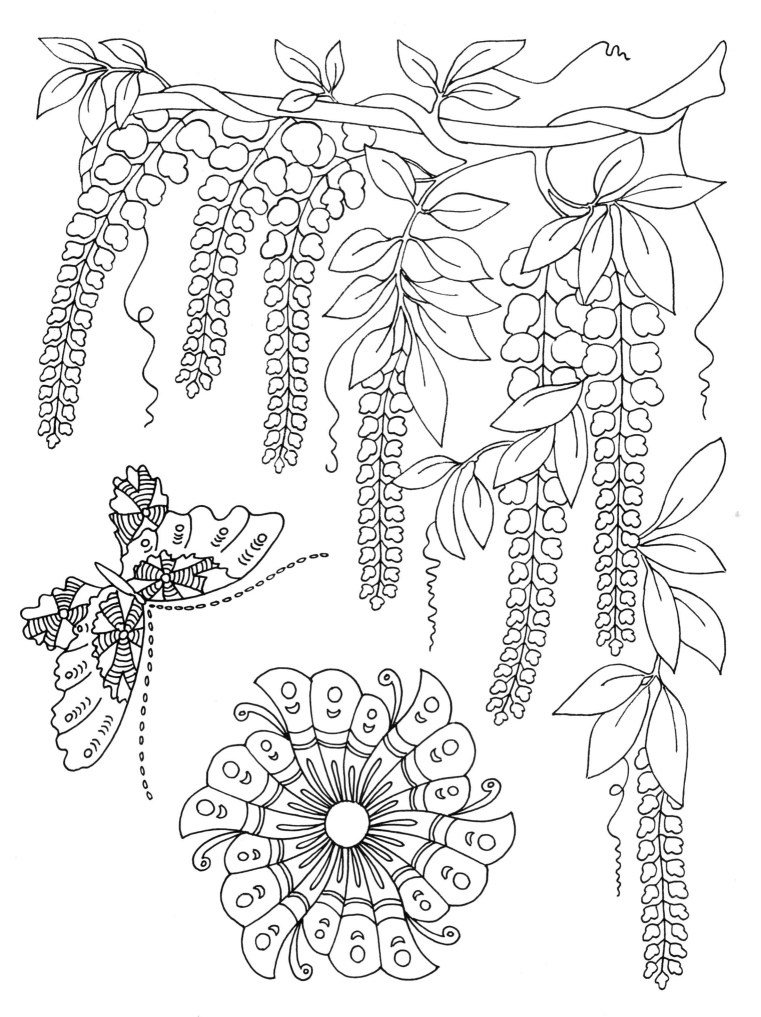